D0064886

PRAYING
THE
PRAYERS
OF THE
BIBLE

FOR YOUR EVERYDAY NEEDS

JAMES BANKS

Discovery House.
from Our Daily Bread Ministries

Praying the Prayers of the Bible for Your Everyday Needs

© 2013, 2018 by James Banks

Discovery House is affiliated with Our Daily Bread Ministries, Grand Rapids, Michigan.

Requests for permission to quote from this book should be directed to: Permissions Department, Discovery House, P.O. Box 3566, Grand Rapids, MI 49501, or contact us by email at permissionsdept@dhp.org.

Interior design by Rob Williams, InsideOutCreativeArts.com

Printed in the United States of America
First printing in 2018

FOR THE FAITHFUL AT PEACE CHURCH

Your love has given me much joy
and comfort, . . .
for your kindness has often
refreshed the hearts of God's people.

PHILEMON 1:7

Contents

PRAYERS FOR SAYING YOU'RE SORRY.......101

PRAYERS FOR FINDING STRENGTH..........119

How to Use This Book

Imagine for a moment that you could actually pray with Moses about gaining a closer relationship with God. Now picture yourself praising God with King David or falling to your knees beside Daniel. Imagine going deeper in your faith as you kneel quietly beside the prophet Isaiah or as you lift your hands toward heaven with Jeremiah as they call on the Lord. Better yet, imagine Jesus standing beside you and helping you learn how to pray.

That's what happens when you pray the prayers of Scripture. You find yourself praying alongside Jesus, Moses, David, Daniel, and others—discovering new strength and encouragement as you do.

God's Spirit moves through His Word in a unique way to speak to us and give us the help and wisdom we need for every day. Tucked neatly away in the pages of Scripture are prayers that apply to life in the most practical ways. As you explore this book, you'll find prayers to help you express your love for God and prayers that show you how to talk with Him about your sins. You'll discover that there are other prayers to encourage you when you're worried about finances or simply concerned about trying to do the right thing.

You'll also find prayers to help you learn how to listen to God or how to pray for those you love. God has included these prayers in His Word for a reason: they draw us out of ourselves and deeper into relationship with Him. In this book you'll find them compiled conveniently to assist you in accessing them easily and in using them day after day. These are prayers that can give your own prayers wings as our heavenly Father carries you to new places of grace.

The best reason for learning how to pray the prayers of the Bible is that Jesus did it. You see this in His final moments on the cross. When He cries, "My God, my God, why have you forsaken me?" (Matthew 27:46), He's praying the first verse of Psalm 22. And when He calls out, "Father, into your hands I commit my spirit" (Luke 23:46 NIV), He's praying from Psalm 31:5. Jesus used the Word of God and Scripture's prayers to help Him as He prayed throughout

His life on earth, and He set the example for us in making it a consistent practice.

Praying the Prayers of the Bible for Your Everyday Needs is divided into several practical sections. They are Prayers for Praising, Saying Thank You, Drawing Near, Saying You're Sorry, Finding Strength, Help, and Blessings. In each of these sections you'll find headings that categorize the prayers into specific topics. For example, in the Prayers for Finding Strength section, you'll encounter "When You Need to Know God Cares for You," "When You're Discouraged," and "When You're Thankful to Be Alive." Each topical arrangement contains several prayers, beginning with longer passages and concluding with shorter ones. You are encouraged to read all the prayers for each category because they provide additional scriptural breadth, and they flow well together.

Several translations of Scripture have been used to compile this book. As in my previous book *Praying the Prayers of the Bible*, the majority of verses have been drawn from the New Living Translation. Every effort has been made to stay faithful to each prayer's original scriptural context and intention. In a few instances, prayers have been combined from different passages that share the same theme. An asterisk (*) beside a prayer reference indicates that the pronouns in the Scripture passage have been changed to help you personally apply the prayer.

May God use this book to draw you near to himself and to give you "eternal encouragement" (2 Thessalonians 2:16 NIV) as you pray. "To him who is able to keep you from stumbling and to present you before his glorious presence without fault and with great joy—to the only God our Savior be glory, majesty, power and authority, through Jesus Christ our Lord, before all ages, now and forevermore! Amen" (Jude 1:24–25 NIV).

Prayers for Praising

When You Want to Draw Closer to God

O God, you are my God; I earnestly search
for you. My soul thirsts for you; my whole
body longs for you in this parched and weary
land where there is no water. I have seen you
in your sanctuary and gazed upon your power
and glory. Your unfailing love is better than life
itself; how I praise you! I will praise you as long
as I live, lifting up my hands to you in prayer.
You satisfy me more than the richest feast.
I will praise you with songs of joy.
I lie awake thinking of you, meditating
on you through the night.

PSALM 63:1–6

My heart has heard you say,
"Come and talk with me." And my heart
responds, "LORD, I am coming."

PSALM 27:8

All praise to God, the Father of our
Lord Jesus Christ. You are our merciful Father
and the source of all comfort.

2 CORINTHIANS 1:3*

Praise the Lord; praise God our savior!
For each day you carry us in your arms.

PSALM 68:19*

When You Want to Praise God More

Let all that I am praise the LORD;
with my whole heart, I will praise your holy
name. Let all that I am praise the LORD;
may I never forget the good things you do for me.
You forgive all my sins and heal all my diseases.
You redeem me from death and crown me with
love and tender mercies. You fill my life with
good things. My youth is renewed
like the eagle's!

PSALM 103:1–5*

Unseal my lips, O Lord,
that my mouth may praise you.

PSALM 51:15

May all who search for you be filled with joy
and gladness in you. May those who love your
salvation repeatedly shout, "The LORD is great!"

PSALM 40:16

All praise to you, the Father of our Lord
Jesus Christ, who has blessed us with every
spiritual blessing in the heavenly realms
because we are united with Christ.

EPHESIANS 1:3*

When You Want to Tell God You Love Him

I love you, LORD; you are my strength.
The LORD is my rock, my fortress, and my
savior; my God is my rock, in whom I find
protection. You are my shield, the power
that saves me, and my place of safety.

PSALM 18:1–2*

As for me, I will sing about your power.
Each morning I will sing with joy about your
unfailing love. For you have been my refuge,
a place of safety when I am in distress.
O my Strength, to you I sing praises, for you,
O God, are my refuge, the God who
shows me unfailing love.

PSALM 59:16–17

I will praise you, LORD, with all my heart;
I will tell of all the marvelous things you
have done. I will be filled with joy because
of you. I will sing praises to your name,
O Most High.

PSALM 9:1-2

Yours, O LORD, is the greatness, the power,
the glory, the victory, and the majesty.
Everything in the heavens and on earth is
yours, O LORD, and this is your kingdom.
We adore you as the one who is over all things.

1 CHRONICLES 29:11

Lord, you know everything;
you know that I love you.

JOHN 21:17 ESV

When God Amazes You

When I consider your heavens, the work of
your fingers, the moon and the stars, which
you have set in place, what is mankind that
you are mindful of them, human beings that
you care for them? You have made them a little
lower than the angels and crowned them with
glory and honor. You made them rulers over
the works of your hands; you put everything
under their feet: all flocks and herds, and the
animals of the wild, the birds in the sky,
and the fish in the sea, all that swim the paths
of the seas. LORD, our Lord, how majestic
is your name in all the earth!

PSALM 8:3–9 NIV

O LORD my God, you have performed many
wonders for me. Your plans for me are too
numerous to list. You have no equal. If I tried
to recite all your wonderful deeds, I would
never come to the end of them.

PSALM 40:5*

Praise the LORD God, the God of Israel,
who alone does such wonderful things.
Praise your glorious name forever!
Let the whole earth be filled with your glory.
Amen and amen!

PSALM 72:18–19*

How awesome are your deeds! Your enemies
cringe before your mighty power. Everything
on earth will worship you; they will sing your
praises, shouting your name in glorious songs.

PSALM 66:3–4

When You Want to Praise God for All He Has Made

Let all that I am praise the LORD. O LORD my God, how great you are! You are robed with honor and majesty. You clothed the earth with floods of water, water that covered even the mountains. At your command, the water fled; at the sound of your thunder, it hurried away. Mountains rose and valleys sank to the levels you decreed. You send rain on the mountains from your heavenly home, and you fill the earth with the fruit of your labor. You cause grass to grow for the livestock and plants for people to use. You allow them to produce food from the earth—wine to make them glad, olive oil to soothe their skin, and bread to give them strength. You made the moon to mark the seasons, and the sun knows when to set.

PSALM 104:1, 6–8, 13–15, 19

Your eternal word, O LORD,
stands firm in heaven. Your faithfulness extends
to every generation, as enduring as
the earth you created.

PSALM 119:89-90

The heavens are yours, and the earth
is yours; everything in the world is yours—
you created it all.

PSALM 89:11

O LORD, our Lord, your majestic name
fills the earth! Your glory is higher than
the heavens.

PSALM 8:1

When You Need to Remember That Everything You Have Comes from God

Wealth and honor come from you alone,
for you rule over everything. Power and might
are in your hand, and at your discretion people
are made great and given strength. O our God,
we thank you and praise your glorious name!
But who am I, and who are my people, that
we could give anything to you? Everything we
have has come from you, and we give you
only what you first gave us!

1 CHRONICLES 29:12–14

Give me an eagerness for your laws rather than
a love for money! Turn my eyes from worthless
things, and give me life through your word.

PSALM 119:36–37

The eyes of all look to you in hope; you give
them their food as they need it. When you
open your hand, you satisfy the hunger and
thirst of every living thing. You are righteous in
everything you do; you are filled with kindness.

PSALM 145:15–17*

I came naked from my mother's womb,
and I will be naked when I leave. The LORD
gave me what I had, and the LORD has taken it
away. Praise the name of the LORD!

JOB 1:21

When You Want to Tell God How Great He Is

I will exalt you, my God the King; I will praise your name for ever and ever. Every day I will praise you and extol your name for ever and ever. Great is the LORD and most worthy of praise; his greatness no one can fathom. One generation commends your works to another; they tell of your mighty acts. They speak of the glorious splendor of your majesty—and I will meditate on your wonderful works. They tell of the power of your awesome works—and I will proclaim your great deeds. They celebrate your abundant goodness and joyfully sing of your righteousness.

PSALM 145:1–7 NIV

For You, LORD, are the Most High over all the earth; You are exalted above all the gods.

PSALM 97:9 HCSB

You are my God, and I will praise you!
You are my God, and I will exalt you!

PSALM 118:28

Great and amazing are your deeds, O Lord
God the Almighty! Just and true are your ways,
O King of the nations! Who will not fear,
O Lord, and glorify your name? For you alone
are holy. All nations will come and worship
you, for your righteous acts have been revealed.

REVELATION 15:3–5 ESV

When You Want to Remember How God Helped You in the Past

Let my soul be at rest again, for the LORD has been good to me. He has saved me from death, my eyes from tears, my feet from stumbling. And so I walk in the LORD's presence as I live here on earth! I believed in you, so I said, "I am deeply troubled, LORD." What can I offer the LORD for all he has done for me? I will lift up the cup of salvation and praise the LORD's name for saving me.

PSALM 116:7–10, 12–13

Who am I, O Sovereign LORD, and what is my
family, that you have brought me this far?

2 SAMUEL 7:18

Praise the LORD, for he has shown me
the wonders of his unfailing love.

PSALM 31:21

You are a God of forgiveness,
gracious and merciful, slow to become angry,
and rich in unfailing love.

NEHEMIAH 9:17

O LORD, I will honor and praise your name, for you
are my God. You do such wonderful things!

ISAIAH 25:1

When You Want to Proclaim God's Glory

Now all glory to God, who is able to keep us
from falling away and will bring us with great
joy into his glorious presence without a single
fault. All glory to you who alone are God,
our Savior through Jesus Christ our Lord.
All glory, majesty, power, and authority are
yours before all time, and in the present,
and beyond all time! Amen.

JUDE 1:24–25*

Glory to God in highest heaven, and peace on
earth to those with whom God is pleased.

LUKE 2:14

May all the kings of the earth praise you, LORD,
when they hear what you have decreed.
May they sing of the ways of the LORD,
for the glory of the LORD is great.

PSALM 138:4–5 NIV

Who is the King of glory? The LORD of
Heaven's Armies—he is the King of glory.

PSALM 24:10

Father, bring glory to your name.

JOHN 12:28

All glory and power to you forever and ever!

1 PETER 4:11*

When You Want to Praise Jesus's Worth

You were slain, and with your blood you
purchased for God persons from every tribe
and language and people and nation.
You have made them to be a kingdom and
priests to serve our God, and they will reign on
the earth. Worthy is the Lamb, who was slain,
to receive power and wealth and wisdom and
strength and honor and glory and praise!
To him who sits on the throne and to the
Lamb be praise and honor and glory and
power, for ever and ever!

REVELATION 5:9-10, 12-13 NIV

Praise God! Blessings on the one who comes in
the name of the Lord! Hail to the King of Israel!

JOHN 12:13

Glorify your Son so he can give glory back to
you. For you have given him authority over
everyone. He gives eternal life to each one you
have given him. And this is the way to have
eternal life—to know you, the only true God,
and Jesus Christ, the one you sent to earth.

JOHN 17:1–3

The world has now become the Kingdom of our
Lord and of his Christ, and he will reign forever
and ever. We give thanks to you, Lord God,
the Almighty, the one who is and who always was,
for now you have assumed your great power
and have begun to reign.

REVELATION 11:15, 17

When You Want to Praise God's Holiness

Holy, holy, holy is the Lord Almighty;
the whole earth is full of his glory.

ISAIAH 6:3 NIV

Your throne, O LORD, has stood from time
immemorial. You yourself are from the
everlasting past. The floods have risen up,
O LORD. The floods have roared like thunder;
the floods have lifted their pounding waves.
But mightier than the violent raging of the
seas, mightier than the breakers on the shore—
the LORD above is mightier than these!
Your royal laws cannot be changed. Your reign,
O LORD, is holy forever and ever.

PSALM 93:2–5

No pagan god is like you, O Lord. None can
do what you do! All the nations you made
will come and bow before you, Lord; they will
praise your holy name. For you are great and
perform wonderful deeds. You alone are God.

PSALM 86:8–10

Let me praise your great and awesome name.
Your name is holy! Mighty King,
lover of justice, you have established fairness.
You have acted with justice.

PSALM 99:3–4*

Holy, holy, holy is the Lord God,
the Almighty—the one who always was,
who is, and who is still to come.

REVELATION 4:8

When You Want to Praise God for His Majesty Shown in Nature

You are dressed in a robe of light. You stretch
out the starry curtain of the heavens;
you lay out the rafters of your home in the rain
clouds. You make the clouds your chariot;
you ride upon the wings of the wind.
The winds are your messengers; flames of
fire are your servants. You placed the world
on its foundation so it would never be moved.
May the glory of the LORD continue forever!
The LORD takes pleasure in all he has made!

PSALM 104:2–5, 31

You, O God, are my king from ages past,
bringing salvation to the earth. Both day and
night belong to you; you made the starlight
and the sun. You set the boundaries of the
earth, and you made both summer and winter.

PSALM 74:12, 16–17

You are glorious and more majestic than
the everlasting mountains.

PSALM 76:4

Be exalted, O God, above the highest heavens!
May your glory shine over all the earth.

PSALM 57:5

When You Want to Praise God for His Word

Your instructions are perfect, reviving the soul.
Your decrees are trustworthy, making wise
the simple. Your commandments are right,
bringing joy to the heart. Your commands are
clear, giving insight for living. Reverence for the
LORD is pure, lasting forever. The laws of the
LORD are true; each one is fair. They are more
desirable than gold, even the finest gold.
They are sweeter than honey, even honey
dripping from the comb. They are a warning to
your servant, a great reward for those
who obey them.

PSALM 19:7–11*

I rejoice in your word like one who
discovers a great treasure.

PSALM 119:162

To all perfection I see a limit, but your
commands are boundless.

PSALM 119:96 NIV

Oh, how I love your instructions! I think
about them all day long. I have refused to
walk on any evil path, so that I may remain
obedient to your word. I haven't turned away
from your regulations, for you have taught
me well. How sweet your words taste to me;
they are sweeter than honey.

PSALM 119:97, 101–103

Your word is truth.

JOHN 17:17 NIV

When You Want to Praise God for Helping You

In my distress I cried out to the LORD; yes, I prayed to my God for help. He heard me from his sanctuary; my cry to him reached his ears. You reached down from heaven and rescued me; you drew me out of deep waters. The LORD lives! Praise to my Rock! May the God of my salvation be exalted!

PSALM 18:6, 16*, 46

Praise the LORD! Give thanks to the LORD, for he is good! His faithful love endures forever. Who can list the glorious miracles of the LORD? Who can ever praise him enough?

PSALM 106:1–2

Because you are my helper, I sing for joy in the
shadow of your wings. I cling to you;
your strong right hand holds me securely.

PSALM 63:7–8

Give thanks to the LORD, for he is good;
his love endures forever. The LORD is with me;
I will not be afraid. What can mere mortals do
to me? The LORD is with me; he is my helper.
I look in triumph on my enemies.

PSALM 118:1, 6–7 NIV

Prayers for Saying Thank You

When You Want to Thank God for Being Faithful

I will sing of the LORD's unfailing love forever!
Young and old will hear of your faithfulness.
Your unfailing love will last forever.
Your faithfulness is as enduring as the heavens.
All heaven will praise your great wonders,
LORD; myriads of angels will praise you for
your faithfulness. For who in all of heaven can
compare with the LORD? What mightiest angel
is anything like the LORD? The highest angelic
powers stand in awe of God. You are far more
awesome than all who surround your throne.
O LORD God of Heaven's Armies! Where is
there anyone as mighty as you, O LORD? You
are entirely faithful.

PSALM 89:1-2, 5-8*

It is good to give thanks to the LORD,
to sing praises to the Most High. It is good to
proclaim your unfailing love in the morning,
your faithfulness in the evening. You thrill me,
LORD, with all you have done for me! I sing for
joy because of what you have done. O LORD,
what great works you do! And how deep
are your thoughts.

PSALM 92:1–2, 4–5

I give you thanks, O LORD, with all my heart;
I praise your name for your unfailing love and
faithfulness; for your promises are backed by
all the honor of your name.

PSALM 138:1–2

When You're Thankful to Be Alive

You made all the delicate, inner parts of my body and knit me together in my mother's womb. Thank you for making me so wonderfully complex! Your workmanship is marvelous—how well I know it. You watched me as I was being formed in utter seclusion, as I was woven together in the dark of the womb. You saw me before I was born. Every day of my life was recorded in your book. Every moment was laid out before a single day had passed. How precious are your thoughts about me, O God. They cannot be numbered! I can't even count them; they outnumber the grains of sand! And when I wake up, you are still with me!

PSALM 139:13–18

I am like an olive tree, thriving in the house of
God. I will always trust in God's unfailing love.
I will praise you forever, O God, for what you
have done. I will trust in your good name in
the presence of your faithful people.

PSALM 52:8–9

LORD, you alone are my inheritance,
my cup of blessing. You guard all that is mine.
What a wonderful inheritance!

PSALM 16:5–6

You are worthy, O Lord our God,
to receive glory and honor and power.
For you created all things, and they exist
because you created what you pleased.

REVELATION 4:11

When You're Thankful for Your Salvation

Praise the Lord, the God of Israel, because he has visited and redeemed his people. You have sent us a mighty Savior from the royal line of your servant David, just as you promised through your holy prophets long ago. We have been rescued from our enemies so we can serve God without fear, in holiness and righteousness for as long as we live.

LUKE 1:68–70, 74–75*

Praise God for the Son of David! Blessings on the one who comes in the name of the LORD! Praise God in highest heaven!

MATTHEW 21:9

Jesus, you gave your life for our sins, just as God our Father planned, in order to rescue us from this evil world in which we live. All glory to God forever and ever! Amen.

GALATIANS 1:4–5*

Salvation comes from our God who sits on the throne and from the Lamb! Amen! Blessing and glory and wisdom and thanksgiving and honor and power and strength belong to our God forever and ever!

REVELATION 7:10, 12

When You Want to Thank God for Your Blessings

You are merciful and compassionate,
slow to get angry and filled with unfailing love.
You are good to everyone. You shower
compassion on all your creation. All of your
works will thank you, LORD, and your faithful
followers will praise you. They will speak of the
glory of your kingdom; they will give examples
of your power. They will tell about your mighty
deeds and about the majesty and glory of your
reign. For your kingdom is an everlasting
kingdom. You rule throughout all generations.

PSALM 145:8-13*

Let all who take refuge in you rejoice;
let them sing joyful praises forever. Spread your
protection over them, that all who love your
name may be filled with joy. For you bless the
godly, O LORD; you surround them with
your shield of love.

PSALM 5:11–12

How great is the goodness you have stored up
for those who fear you. You lavish it on those
who come to you for protection, blessing them
before the watching world.

PSALM 31:19

You have endowed me with eternal blessings
and given me the joy of your presence.

PSALM 21:6*

When You're Grateful for Answered Prayer

You faithfully answer our prayers with awesome deeds, O God our savior. You are the hope of everyone on earth, even those who sail on distant seas. You formed the mountains by your power and armed yourself with mighty strength. You quieted the raging oceans with their pounding waves and silenced the shouting of the nations. Those who live at the ends of the earth stand in awe of your wonders. From where the sun rises to where it sets, you inspire shouts of joy.

PSALM 65:5–8

I thank you for answering my prayer
and giving me victory!

PSALM 118:21

Father, thank you for hearing me.
You always hear me.

JOHN 11:41–42

Now all glory to you, who are able, through
your mighty power at work within us,
to accomplish infinitely more than we might
ask or think. Glory to you in the church
and in Christ Jesus through all generations
forever and ever! Amen.

EPHESIANS 3:20–21*

When You Want to Thank God for His Wisdom

Praise the name of God forever and ever,
for you have all wisdom and power.
You control the course of world events;
you remove kings and set up other kings.
You give wisdom to the wise and knowledge to
the scholars. You reveal deep and mysterious
things and know what lies hidden in darkness,
though you are surrounded by light. I thank
and praise you, God of my ancestors, for you
have given me wisdom and strength.

DANIEL 2:20–23*

LORD, there is no one like you! For you are
great, and your name is full of power.
Who would not fear you, O King of nations?
That title belongs to you alone!
Among all the wise people of the earth
and in all the kingdoms of the world,
there is no one like you.

JEREMIAH 10:6–7

O Father, Lord of heaven and earth,
thank you for hiding these things from those
who think themselves wise and clever, and for
revealing them to the childlike. Yes, Father,
it pleased you to do it this way!

MATTHEW 11:25–26

All glory to the only wise God,
through Jesus Christ, forever. Amen.

ROMANS 16:27

When God Has Rescued You from Harm

I will rejoice because you have rescued me. I will sing to the LORD because he is good to me. I will praise your name, O LORD, for it is good. For you have rescued me from my troubles and helped me to triumph over my enemies. Praise the LORD! For he has heard my cry for mercy. The LORD is my strength and shield. I trust him with all my heart. He helps me, and my heart is filled with joy. I burst out in songs of thanksgiving.

PSALM 13:5–6; 54:6–7; 28:6–7

In my alarm I said, "I am cut off from
your sight." Yet you heard my cry for mercy
when I call to you for help.

PSALM 31:22 NIV

My heart rejoices in the LORD! The LORD has
made me strong. Now I have an answer for
my enemies; I rejoice because you rescued me.
No one is holy like the LORD! There is no one
besides you; there is no Rock like our God.

1 SAMUEL 2:1–2

Sing to the LORD! Praise the LORD!
For though I was poor and needy,
you rescued me from my oppressors.

JEREMIAH 20:13*

When You Want to Thank God for His Love

My heart is confident in you, O God;
my heart is confident. No wonder I can sing
your praises! Wake up, my heart! Wake up,
O lyre and harp! I will wake the dawn with
my song. I will thank you, Lord, among all
the people. I will sing your praises among the
nations. For your unfailing love is as high as the
heavens. Your faithfulness reaches to
the clouds. Be exalted, O God, above the
highest heavens. May your glory shine over
all the earth.

PSALM 57:7–11

With your unfailing love you lead the people
you have redeemed. In your might,
you guide me to your sacred home.

EXODUS 15:13*

Oh, how my soul praises the Lord.
How my spirit rejoices in God my Savior!
For the Mighty One is holy, and he has done
great things for me.

LUKE 1:46–47, 49

Power, O God, belongs to you; unfailing love,
O Lord, is yours.

PSALM 62:11–12

When You Want to Thank God for a Victory

You light a lamp for me. The LORD, my God,
lights up my darkness. Your way is perfect.
All the LORD's promises prove true. You are a
shield for all who look to you for protection.
For who is God except the LORD? Who but our
God is a solid rock? You arm me with strength,
and you make my way perfect. You make me
as surefooted as a deer, enabling me to stand
on mountain heights. You have given me your
shield of victory. Your right hand supports me;
your help has made me great. You have
made a wide path for my feet to keep them
from slipping.

PSALM 18:28, 30–33, 35–36*

The LORD is my strength and my song;
you have given me victory. You are my God,
and I will praise you—my father's God,
and I will exalt you! The LORD is a warrior;
Yahweh is his name!

EXODUS 15:2–3*

I will exalt you, LORD, for you rescued me.
You refused to let my enemies triumph over
me. You have turned my mourning into joyful
dancing. You have taken away my clothes
of mourning and clothed me with joy,
that I might sing praises to you and not be
silent. O LORD my God, I will give you
thanks forever!

PSALM 30:1, 11–12

Prayers for
Drawing Near

When You Long to Be with God

How lovely is your dwelling place, O LORD of Heaven's Armies. I long, yes, I faint with longing to enter the courts of the LORD. With my whole being, body and soul, I will shout joyfully to the living God. Even the sparrow finds a home, and the swallow builds her nest and raises her young at a place near your altar, O LORD of Heaven's Armies, my King and my God! What joy for those who can live in your house, always singing your praises. What joy for those whose strength comes from the LORD.

PSALM 84:1–5

You guide me with your counsel, and afterward you will receive me to glory. Whom have I in heaven but you? And there is nothing on earth that I desire besides you. My flesh and my heart may fail, but God is the strength of my heart and my portion forever.

PSALM 73:24–26 ESV

O LORD, come back to me! How long will you delay? Take pity on your servant! Satisfy me each morning with your unfailing love, so I may sing for joy to the end of my life.

PSALM 90:13–14*

Show me your glorious presence.

EXODUS 33:18

When You Want God More Than Anything

Whom have I in heaven but you? I desire you more than anything on earth. My health may fail, and my spirit may grow weak, but you remain the strength of my heart; you are mine forever. Those who desert you will perish, for you destroy those who abandon you. But as for me, how good it is to be near you! I have made the Sovereign LORD my shelter, and I will tell everyone about the wonderful things you do.

PSALM 73:25–28*

As the deer longs for streams of water, so I long
for you, O God. I thirst for God, the living
God. When can I go and stand before you?

PSALM 42:1–2*

You do not desire a sacrifice,
or I would offer one. You do not want a
burnt offering. The sacrifice you desire
is a broken spirit. You will not reject
a broken and repentant heart, O God.

PSALM 51:16–17

Search me, O God, and know my heart;
test me and know my anxious thoughts.
Point out anything in me that offends you,
and lead me along the path of everlasting life.

PSALM 139:23–24

When You Need to Find Peace

The Lord is my shepherd; I have all that
I need. You let me rest in green meadows;
    you lead me beside peaceful streams.
You renew my strength. You guide me along
    right paths, bringing honor to your name.
Even when I walk through the darkest valley,
I will not be afraid, for you are close beside me.
Your rod and your staff protect and comfort
me. You prepare a feast for me in the presence
of my enemies. You honor me by anointing my
head with oil. My cup overflows with blessings.
    Surely your goodness and unfailing love
will pursue me all the days of my life, and I will
    live in the house of the Lord forever.

PSALM 23:1–6*

You will keep in perfect peace all who trust in
you, all whose thoughts are fixed on you!

ISAIAH 26:3

Those who love your instructions have great
peace and do not stumble.

PSALM 119:165

Many people say, "Who will show us better
times?" Let your face smile on us, LORD.
You have given me greater joy than those
who have abundant harvests of grain and new
wine. In peace I will lie down and sleep,
for you alone, O LORD, will keep me safe.

PSALM 4:6–8

When You Need an Eternal Perspective

LORD, remind me how brief my time on earth will be. Remind me that my days are numbered—how fleeting my life is. You have made my life no longer than the width of my hand. My entire lifetime is just a moment to you; at best, each of us is but a breath. We are merely moving shadows, and all our busy rushing ends in nothing. We heap up wealth, not knowing who will spend it. And so, Lord, where do I put my hope? My only hope is in you.

PSALM 39:4–7

You alone can never die, and you live in light so brilliant that no human can approach you. No human eye has ever seen you, nor ever will. All honor and power to you forever!

1 TIMOTHY 6:16*

We are here for only a moment, visitors and
strangers in the land as our ancestors were
before us. Our days on earth are like a passing
shadow, gone so soon without a trace.

1 CHRONICLES 29:15

O LORD, what are human beings that
you should notice them, mere mortals
that you should think about them? For we are
like a breath of air; our days are like
a passing shadow.

PSALM 144:3–4*

Be good to your servant while I live,
that I may obey your word. Open my eyes that
I may see wonderful things in your law.
I am a stranger on earth.

PSALM 119:17–19 NIV

Teach me to realize the brevity of life,
so that I may grow in wisdom.

PSALM 90:12*

When You Need Encouragement to Pray

You always keep your promises; you are
gracious in all you do. You help the fallen and
lift those bent beneath their loads. You are
close to all who call on you, yes, to all who call
on you in truth. You grant the desires of those
who fear you; you hear their cries for help and
rescue them. You protect all those who love
you, but you destroy the wicked. I will praise
the LORD, and may everyone on earth bless
your holy name forever and ever.

PSALM 145:13–14, 18–21*

Prayers for Drawing Near

Since ancient times no one has heard, no ear has perceived, no eye has seen any God besides you, who acts on behalf of those who wait for him.

ISAIAH 64:4 NIV

Answer my prayers, O LORD, for your unfailing love is wonderful. Take care of me, for your mercy is so plentiful.

PSALM 69:16

In my distress I called to the LORD, and he answered me. From deep in the realm of the dead I called for help, and you listened to my cry.

JONAH 2:2 NIV

As soon as I pray, you answer me; you encourage me by giving me strength.

PSALM 138:3

When You Need to Be Still before God

If you, LORD, kept a record of sins, Lord,
who could stand? But with you there is
forgiveness, so that we can, with reverence,
serve you. I wait for the LORD, my whole being
waits, and in his word I put my hope. I wait
for the Lord more than watchmen wait for the
morning, more than watchmen wait for the
morning. I lift up my eyes to you, to you who
sit enthroned in heaven. As the eyes of slaves
look to the hand of their master, as the eyes of
a female slave look to the hand of her mistress,
so our eyes look to the LORD our God,
till he shows us his mercy.

PSALM 130:3–6; 123:1–2 NIV

My heart is not proud, LORD, my eyes
are not haughty; I do not concern myself with
great matters or things too wonderful for me.
But I have calmed and quieted myself,
I am like a weaned child with its mother;
like a weaned child I am content.

PSALM 131:1–2 NIV

Let all that I am wait quietly before God,
for my hope is in him. You alone are my rock
and my salvation, my fortress where I will not
be shaken. My victory and honor come from
God alone. You are my refuge, a rock where
no enemy can reach me.

PSALM 62:5–7*

Speak, LORD, for your servant is listening.

1 SAMUEL 3:9 NIV

When You Want to Pray for God's Kingdom to Come

Our Father in heaven, may your name be kept holy. May your Kingdom come soon. May your will be done on earth, as it is in heaven. Give us today the food we need, and forgive us our sins, as we have forgiven those who sin against us. And don't let us yield to temptation, but rescue us from the evil one.

MATTHEW 6:9–13

Blessings on the King who comes in the name of the Lord! Peace in heaven, and glory in highest heaven!

LUKE 19:38

Rise up, O God, and judge the earth,
for all the nations belong to you.

PSALM 82:8

All honor and glory to God forever and ever!
You are the eternal King, the unseen one who
never dies; you alone are God.

1 TIMOTHY 1:17*

All glory to you who love us and have freed us
from our sins by shedding your blood for us.
You have made us a Kingdom of priests for
God your Father. All glory and power to you
forever and ever! Amen.

REVELATION 1:5–6*

Come, Lord Jesus!

REVELATION 22:20 ESV

When You Want to Grow in Faith

I pray that my heart will be flooded with light
so that I can understand the confident hope
you have given to those you called—
your holy people who are your rich and glorious
inheritance. I also pray that I will understand
the incredible greatness of God's power for
us who believe you. This is the same mighty
power that raised Christ from the dead and
seated him in the place of honor at God's right
hand in the heavenly realms. Now he is far
above any ruler or authority or power or leader
or anything else—not only in this world but
also in the world to come.

EPHESIANS 1:18–21*

I do believe,
but help me overcome my unbelief!

MARK 9:24

O Sovereign Lord, you have only begun to
show your greatness and the strength of your
hand to me, your servant. Is there any god in
heaven or on earth who can perform such
great and mighty deeds as you do?

DEUTERONOMY 3:24

Show me how to increase my faith.

LUKE 17:5*

When You Want to Declare Your Dependence on God

I will proclaim your name to my brothers and sisters. I will praise you among your assembled people. Praise the LORD, all you who fear him! Honor him, all you descendants of Jacob! Show him reverence, all you descendants of Israel! For he has not ignored or belittled the suffering of the needy. He has not turned his back on them, but has listened to their cries for help.

PSALM 22:22–24

Only by your power can we push back our
enemies; only in your name can we trample
our foes. I do not trust in my bow; I do not
count on my sword to save me. O God,
we give glory to you all day long and
constantly praise your name.

PSALM 44:5–6, 8

Not to me, O LORD, not to me,
but to your name goes all the glory for your
unfailing love and faithfulness.

PSALM 115:1*

As your name deserves, O God, you will be
praised to the ends of the earth. Your strong
right hand is filled with victory.

PSALM 48:10

You are my Lord; apart from you
I have no good thing.

PSALM 16:2 NIV

When You Want to Serve God

For those who are righteous, the way is not steep and rough. You are a God who does what is right, and you smooth out the path ahead of them. LORD, I show my trust in you by obeying your laws; my heart's desire is to glorify your name. In the night I search for you; in the morning I earnestly seek you. For only when you come to judge the earth will people learn what is right. Your kindness to the wicked does not make them do good. Although others do right, the wicked keep doing wrong and take no notice of your majesty. LORD, you will grant me peace; all I have accomplished is really from you.

ISAIAH 26:7–10, 12*

I am at your command.
What do you want your servant to do?

JOSHUA 5:14

I take joy in doing your will, my God,
for your instructions are written on my heart.

PSALM 40:8

You have charged us to keep your
commandments carefully. Oh, that my actions
would consistently reflect your decrees!
As I learn your righteous regulations,
I will thank you by living as I should!

PSALM 119:4–5, 7

My Lord and my God!

JOHN 20:28

When You're Looking Forward to Eternity

All praise to you, the Father of our
Lord Jesus Christ. It is by your great mercy
that I have been born again. Now I live
with great expectation, and I have a
priceless inheritance.

1 PETER 1:3–4*

You will swallow up death forever!
The Sovereign LORD will wipe away all tears.
You will remove forever all insults and mockery
against your land and people. The LORD has
spoken! In that day the people will proclaim,
"This is our God! We trusted in him, and he
saved us! This is the LORD, in whom we trusted.
Let us rejoice in the salvation he brings!"

ISAIAH 25:8–9*

Those who die in the LORD will live;
their bodies will rise again! Those who sleep
in the earth will rise up and sing for joy!
For your life-giving light will fall like dew
on your people in the place of the dead!

ISAIAH 26:19

When I awake, I will see you face to face
and be satisfied.

PSALM 17:15

Hallelujah! For our Lord God Almighty reigns.

REVELATION 19:6 NIV

When You Want to Remember God's Lasting Greatness

Long ago you laid the foundation of the earth and made the heavens with your hands. They will perish, but you remain forever; they will wear out like old clothing. You will change them like a garment and discard them. But you are always the same; you will live forever. The children of your people will live in security. Their children's children will thrive in your presence.

PSALM 102:25–28

O LORD, God of our ancestors, you alone are
the God who is in heaven. You are ruler of all
the kingdoms of the earth. You are powerful
and mighty; no one can stand against you!

2 CHRONICLES 20:6

Though the wicked sprout like weeds and
evildoers flourish, they will be destroyed
forever. But you, O LORD, will be exalted
forever. Your enemies, LORD, will surely perish;
all evildoers will be scattered.

PSALM 92:7-9

When You Want to Acknowledge God's Handiwork in Nature

You take care of the earth and water it,
making it rich and fertile. The river of God has
plenty of water; it provides a bountiful harvest
of grain, for you have ordered it so. You drench
the plowed ground with rain, melting the clods
and leveling the ridges. You soften the earth
with showers and bless its abundant crops.
You crown the year with a bountiful harvest;
even the hard pathways overflow with
abundance. The grasslands of the wilderness
become a lush pasture, and the hillsides
blossom with joy. The meadows are clothed
with flocks of sheep, and the valleys are
carpeted with grain. They all shout
and sing for joy!

PSALM 65:9–13

You rule the oceans.
You subdue their storm-tossed waves.

PSALM 89:9

O Lord, what a variety of things you have
made! In wisdom you have made them all.
The earth is full of your creatures.

PSALM 104:24

Truly, O God of Israel, our Savior,
you work in mysterious ways.

ISAIAH 45:15

When You Want to Remember God's Wonder-Working Power

When the Red Sea saw you, O God, its waters looked and trembled! The sea quaked to its very depths. The clouds poured down rain; the thunder rumbled in the sky. Your arrows of lightning flashed. Your thunder roared from the whirlwind; the lightning lit up the world! The earth trembled and shook. Your road led through the sea, your pathway through the mighty waters—a pathway no one knew was there! You led your people along that road like a flock of sheep, with Moses and Aaron as their shepherds.

PSALM 77:16–20

Was it in anger, LORD, that you struck the
rivers and parted the sea? Were you displeased
with them? No, you were sending your chariots
of salvation! You went out to rescue your
chosen people, to save your anointed ones.

HABAKKUK 3:8, 13

The enemy runs at the sound of your voice.
When you stand up, the nations flee!

ISAIAH 33:3

How great you are, O Sovereign LORD!
There is no one like you. We have never even
heard of another God like you!

2 SAMUEL 7:22

When You Need to Remember God's Righteous Anger toward Sin

You turn people back to dust, saying,
"Return to dust, you mortals!" For you,
a thousand years are as a passing day, as brief as
a few night hours. You sweep people away like
dreams that disappear. They are like grass that
springs up in the morning. In the morning it
blooms and flourishes, but by evening it is dry
and withered. We wither beneath your anger;
we are overwhelmed by your fury. You spread
out our sins before you—our secret sins—
and you see them all. We live our lives beneath
your wrath, ending our years with a groan.
Seventy years are given to us! Some even live
to eighty. But even the best years are filled
with pain and trouble; soon they disappear,
and we fly away. Who can comprehend the
power of your anger? Your wrath is as
awesome as the fear you deserve.

PSALM 90:3–11

No wonder you are greatly feared! Who can
stand before you when your anger explodes?
From heaven you sentenced your enemies;
the earth trembled and stood silent before you.
You stand up to judge those who do evil,
O God, and to rescue the oppressed of the
earth. Human defiance only enhances your
glory, for you use it as a weapon.

PSALM 76:7–10

You, O God, will send the wicked down to the
pit of destruction. Murderers and liars will die
young, but I am trusting you to save me.

PSALM 55:23

When You Want to Acknowledge God's Justice and Mercy

May your ways be known throughout the earth, your saving power among people everywhere. May the nations praise you, O God. Yes, may all the nations praise you. Let the whole world sing for joy, because you govern the nations with justice and guide the people of the whole world. May the nations praise you, O God. Yes, may all the nations praise you.

PSALM 67:2–5

Your throne, O God, endures forever and ever.
You rule with a scepter of justice.

PSALM 45:6

Yes, O Lord God, the Almighty,
your judgments are true and just.

REVELATION 16:7

O LORD, I am your servant; yes,
I am your servant, born into your household;
you have freed me from my chains.

PSALM 116:16

When You Long to
See Revival in the Land

You, LORD, showed favor to your land;
you restored the fortunes of Jacob. You forgave
the iniquity of your people and covered all
their sins. You set aside all your wrath and
turned from your fierce anger. Restore us
again, God our Savior, and put away your
displeasure toward us. Will you be angry
with us forever? Will you prolong your anger
through all generations? Will you not revive
us again, that your people may rejoice in you?
Show us your unfailing love, LORD, and grant
us your salvation.

PSALM 85:1–7 NIV

Help, O Lord, for the godly are
fast disappearing! The faithful have
vanished from the earth!

PSALM 12:1

I lie in the dust; revive me by your word.
I weep with sorrow; encourage me by your word.

PSALM 119:25, 28

Revive us so we can call on your name once
more. Turn us again to yourself, O Lord God
of Heaven's Armies. Make your face shine
down upon us. Only then will we be saved.

PSALM 80:18–19

Prayers for Saying You're Sorry

When You've Sinned

Have mercy on me, O God, because of
your unfailing love. Because of your great
compassion, blot out the stain of my sins.
Wash me clean from my guilt. Purify me from
my sin. For I recognize my rebellion; it haunts
me day and night. Against you, and you alone,
have I sinned; I have done what is evil in your
sight. You will be proved right in what you say,
and your judgment against me is just.
For I was born a sinner—yes, from the moment
my mother conceived me. But you desire
honesty from the womb, teaching me
wisdom even there.

PSALM 51:1-6

O God, be merciful to me, for I am a sinner.

LUKE 18:13

My sins pile up so high I can't see my way out.
They outnumber the hairs on my head.
I have lost all courage. Please, LORD, rescue me!
Come quickly, LORD, and help me.

PSALM 40:12–13

For the honor of your name, O LORD,
forgive my many, many sins. Turn to me and
have mercy, for I am alone and in deep distress.
My problems go from bad to worse.
Oh, save me from them all! Feel my pain
and see my trouble. Forgive all my sins.

PSALM 25:11, 16–18

When God Has Disciplined You

You made me; you created me. Now give me
the sense to follow your commands. May all
who fear you find in me a cause for joy,
for I have put my hope in your word. I know,
O LORD, that your regulations are fair;
you disciplined me because I needed it.
Now let your unfailing love comfort me, just as
you promised me, your servant. Surround me
with your tender mercies so I may live,
for your instructions are my delight. Let me be
united with all who fear you, with those who
know your laws. May I be blameless in keeping
your decrees; then I will never be ashamed.

PSALM 119:73–77, 79–80

Have mercy on me, LORD, for I am in distress.
Tears blur my eyes. My body and soul are
withering away. I am dying from grief;
my years are shortened by sadness. Sin has drained
my strength; I am wasting away from within.

PSALM 31:9–10

Forgive all my sins and graciously receive me,
so that I may offer you my praises.

HOSEA 14:2*

Joyful are those you discipline, LORD,
those you teach with your instructions.

PSALM 94:12

When You Need to Be Assured of God's Forgiveness

Oh, what joy for those whose disobedience is forgiven, whose sin is put out of sight! Yes, what joy for those whose record the LORD has cleared of guilt, whose lives are lived in complete honesty! When I refused to confess my sin, my body wasted away, and I groaned all day long. Day and night your hand of discipline was heavy on me. My strength evaporated like water in the summer heat. Finally, I confessed all my sins to you and stopped trying to hide my guilt. I said to myself, "I will confess my rebellion to the LORD." And you forgave me! All my guilt is gone. Therefore, let all the godly pray to you while there is still time, that they may not drown in the floodwaters of judgment. For you are my hiding place; you protect me from trouble. You surround me with songs of victory.

PSALM 32:1–7

If I had not confessed the sin in my heart,
the Lord would not have listened. But God
did listen! He paid attention to my prayer.
Praise God, who did not ignore my prayer or
withdraw his unfailing love from me.

PSALM 66:18–20

Though I am overwhelmed by my sins,
you forgive them all. What joy for those
you choose to bring near, those who live
in your holy Temple.

PSALM 65:3–4*

I will praise you, O LORD! You were angry with
me, but not any more. Now you comfort me.

ISAIAH 12:1

When You Need to Humble Yourself before God

You come to the help of those who gladly do right, who remember your ways. But when we continued to sin against them, you were angry. How then can we be saved? All of us have become like one who is unclean, and all our righteous acts are like filthy rags; we all shrivel up like a leaf, and like the wind our sins sweep us away. No one calls on your name or strives to lay hold of you; for you have hidden your face from us and have given us over to our sins. Yet you, LORD, are our Father. We are the clay, you are the potter; we are all the work of your hand.

ISAIAH 64:5–8 NIV

What more can I say to you? You know what
your servant is really like, Sovereign LORD.

2 SAMUEL 7:20

O God, You know my foolishness;
and my sins are not hidden from you.

PSALM 69:5 NKJV

Every time you punished me you were
being just. I have sinned greatly,
and you gave me only what I deserved.

NEHEMIAH 9:33*

I am unworthy of all the kindness and
faithfulness you have shown your servant.

GENESIS 32:10 NIV

When God Has Corrected You

You have done many good things for me,
LORD, just as you promised. I believe in your
commands; now teach me good judgment
and knowledge. I used to wander off until you
disciplined me; but now I closely follow your
word. You are good and do only good;
teach me your decrees. My suffering was good
for me, for it taught me to pay attention
to your decrees. Your instructions are more
valuable to me than millions in gold and silver.

PSALM 119:65–68, 71–72

I know, Lord, that our lives are not our own.
We are not able to plan our own course.
So correct me, Lord, but please be gentle.
Do not correct me in anger, for I would die.

JEREMIAH 10:23–24

Don't let those who trust in you be ashamed
because of me, O Sovereign LORD of Heaven's
Armies. Don't let me cause them to be
humiliated, O God of Israel.

PSALM 69:6

You have tested me, O God;
you have purified me like silver.

PSALM 66:10*

Lord, your discipline is good, for it leads to
life and health. You restore my health
and allow me to live!

ISAIAH 38:16

When You Need to
Tell God, "I'm Sorry"

O Lord, you are a great and awesome God!
You always fulfill your covenant and keep
your promises of unfailing love to those who
love you and obey your commands.
But I have sinned and done wrong. I have
rebelled against you and scorned your
commands and regulations. Lord, you are
in the right; but as you see, my face is
covered with shame.

DANIEL 9:4–5, 7*

LORD, see my anguish! My heart is broken and my soul despairs, for I have rebelled against you.

LAMENTATIONS 1:20

O my God, I am utterly ashamed;
I blush to lift up my face to you. For my sins
are piled higher than my head, and my guilt
has reached to the heavens.

EZRA 9:6*

Help me, O God of my salvation!
Help me for the glory of your name.
Save me and forgive my sins for the
honor of your name.

PSALM 79:9*

When Your Heart Is Stubborn

LORD, look down from heaven; look from your holy, glorious home, and see me. Where is the passion and the might you used to show on my behalf? Where are your mercy and compassion now? Surely you are still my Father! Even if Abraham and Jacob would disown me, LORD, you would still be my Father. You are my Redeemer from ages past. LORD, why have you allowed me to turn from your path? Why have you given me a stubborn heart so I no longer fear you? Return and help me, for I am your servant.

ISAIAH 63:15–17*

O LORD of Heaven's Armies, you make
righteous judgments, and you examine the
deepest thoughts and secrets.

JEREMIAH 11:20

Restore me, O LORD, and bring me back to
you again! Give me back the joys I once had!

LAMENTATIONS 5:21*

You rescue the humble, but your eyes watch
the proud and humiliate them. O LORD, you
are my lamp. The LORD lights up my darkness.

2 SAMUEL 22:28–29

Have mercy on me, LORD; heal me,
for I have sinned against you.

PSALM 41:4 NIV

When You've Had to Bear the Consequences of Your Sin

Rescue me from my rebellion. Do not let fools mock me. I am silent before you; I won't say a word, for my punishment is from you. But please stop striking me! I am exhausted by the blows from your hand. When you discipline us for our sins, you consume like a moth what is precious to us. Each of us is but a breath. Hear my prayer, O LORD! Listen to my cries for help! Don't ignore my tears. For I am your guest—a traveler passing through, as my ancestors were before me.

PSALM 39:8–12

My guilt overwhelms me—it is a burden too
heavy to bear. I am exhausted and completely
crushed. My groans come from an anguished
heart. You know what I long for, Lord;
you hear my every sigh. But I confess my sins;
I am deeply sorry for what I have done.

PSALM 38:4, 8–9, 18

Purify me from my sins, and I will be clean;
wash me, and I will be whiter than snow.
Oh, give me back my joy again; you have
broken me—now let me rejoice.
Don't keep looking at my sins.
Remove the stain of my guilt.

PSALM 51:7–9

Prayers for Finding Strength

When Times Are Difficult

Your righteousness, God, reaches to the
heavens, you who have done great things.
Who is like you, God? Though you have made
me see troubles, many and bitter, you will restore
my life again; from the depths of the earth you
will again bring me up. You will increase my
honor and comfort me once more. My lips will
shout for joy when I sing praise to you—
I whom you have delivered. My tongue will tell
of your righteous acts all day long.

PSALM 71:19–21, 23–24 NIV

O LORD, God of my salvation, I cry out to you by
day. I come to you at night. Now hear my prayer;
listen to my cry. For my life is full of troubles.

PSALM 88:1–3

Answer me when I call to you, O God who
declares me innocent. Free me from my
troubles. Have mercy on me and hear my prayer.

PSALM 4:1

You are my refuge and my shield;
your word is my source of hope. LORD,
sustain me as you promised, that I may live!
Do not let my hope be crushed.

PSALM 119:114, 116

Why, my soul, are you downcast?
Why so disturbed within me?
Put your hope in God, for I will yet praise him,
my Savior and my God.

PSALM 43:5 NIV

When You're Discouraged

Why am I discouraged? Why is my heart so sad? I will put my hope in God! I will praise him again—my Savior and my God!

Now I am deeply discouraged, but I will remember you. I hear the tumult of the raging seas as your waves and surging tides sweep over me. But each day the LORD pours his unfailing love upon me, and through each night I sing his songs, praying to God who gives me life.

PSALM 42:5–8

From the depths of despair, O LORD,
I call for your help. Hear my cry, O Lord.
Pay attention to my prayer. LORD, if you kept
a record of our sins, who, O Lord, could ever
survive? But you offer forgiveness, that we
might learn to fear you.

PSALM 130:1–4

I cried out, "I am slipping!" but your
unfailing love, O LORD, supported me.
When doubts filled my mind, your comfort
gave me renewed hope and cheer.

PSALM 94:18–19

My eyes are blinded by my tears.
Each day I beg for your help, O LORD;
I lift my hands to you for mercy.

PSALM 88:9

When You Need Assurance

I will bless the LORD who guides me;
even at night my heart instructs me.
I know the LORD is always with me.
I will not be shaken, for he is right beside me.
No wonder my heart is glad, and I rejoice.
My body rests in safety. For you will not leave
my soul among the dead or allow your holy
one to rot in the grave. You will show me the
way of life, granting me the joy of
your presence and the pleasures of
living with you forever.

PSALM 16:7–11

O LORD, God of heaven, the great and
awesome God who keeps his covenant of
unfailing love with those who love him and
obey his commands, listen to my prayer!
Look down and see me praying night and day
for your people Israel. I confess that we have
sinned against you. Yes, even my own family
and I have sinned!

NEHEMIAH 1:5–6

But in your great mercy, you did not destroy
them completely or abandon them forever.
What a gracious and merciful God you are!

NEHEMIAH 9:31

And now, may it please you to bless the house
of your servant, so that it may continue forever
before you. For you have spoken,
and when you grant a blessing to your servant,
O Sovereign LORD, it is an eternal blessing!

2 SAMUEL 7:29

When You Need to Know That God Cares for You

Your unfailing love, O LORD, is as vast as the heavens; your faithfulness reaches beyond the clouds. Your righteousness is like the mighty mountains, your justice like the ocean depths. You care for people and animals alike, O LORD. How precious is your unfailing love, O God! All humanity finds shelter in the shadow of your wings. You feed them from the abundance of your own house, letting them drink from your river of delights. For you are the fountain of life, the light by which we see.

PSALM 36:5–9

Yet this I call to mind and therefore
I have hope: Because of the LORD's great love
we are not consumed, for his compassions
never fail. They are new every morning;
great is your faithfulness.

LAMENTATIONS 3:21–23 NIV

May your glorious name be praised!
May it be exalted above all blessing and praise!
You alone are the LORD. You made the skies
and the heavens and all the stars. You made the
earth and the seas and everything in them.
You preserve them all, and the angels of
heaven worship you.

NEHEMIAH 9:5–6

Those who know your name trust in you,
for you, LORD, have never forsaken those
who seek you.

PSALM 9:10 NIV

When You're Having Trouble Making Ends Meet

Even though the fig trees have no blossoms,
and there are no grapes on the vines;
even though the olive crop fails, and the fields
lie empty and barren; even though the flocks
die in the fields, and the cattle barns are empty,
yet I will rejoice in the LORD! I will be joyful in
the God of my salvation! The Sovereign LORD
is my strength! You make me as surefooted as a
deer, able to tread upon the heights.

HABAKKUK 3:17–19*

O God, I beg two favors from you; let me have
them before I die. First, help me never to tell a
lie. Second, give me neither poverty nor riches!
Give me just enough to satisfy my needs.
For if I grow rich, I may deny you and say,
"Who is the LORD?" And if I am too poor,
I may steal and thus insult God's holy name.

PROVERBS 30:7–9

As for me, since I am poor and needy, let the
Lord keep me in his thoughts. You are my
helper and my savior. O my God, do not delay.

PSALM 40:17

But you are a tower of refuge to the poor,
O LORD, a tower of refuge to the needy in
distress. You are a refuge from the storm
and a shelter from the heat.

ISAIAH 25:4

When You're Struggling with Depression

Bend down, O LORD, and hear my prayer; answer me, for I need your help. Protect me, for I am devoted to you. Save me, for I serve you and trust you. You are my God. Be merciful to me, O Lord, for I am calling on you constantly. Give me happiness, O Lord, for I give myself to you. O Lord, you are so good, so ready to forgive, so full of unfailing love for all who ask for your help. Listen closely to my prayer, O LORD; hear my urgent cry. I will call to you whenever I'm in trouble, and you will answer me.

PSALM 86:1–7

Lord, don't hold back your tender mercies
from me. Let your unfailing love and
faithfulness always protect me. For troubles
surround me—too many to count!

PSALM 40:11–12

Come quickly, Lord, and answer me,
for my depression deepens. Don't turn away
from me. Let me hear of your unfailing love
each morning, for I am trusting you. Show me
where to walk, for I give myself to you.

PSALM 143:7–8

Why am I discouraged? Why is my heart so
sad? I will put my hope in God! I will praise
him again—my Savior and my God!

PSALM 42:11

When Your Heart Is Broken

LORD, hear my prayer! Listen to my plea!
Don't turn away from me in my time of
distress. Bend down to listen, and answer
me quickly when I call to you. For my days
disappear like smoke, and my bones burn like
red-hot coals. My heart is sick, withered like
grass, and I have lost my appetite. Because of
my groaning, I am reduced to skin and bones.
I am like an owl in the desert, like a little owl
in a far-off wilderness. I lie awake, lonely as
a solitary bird on the roof. My life passes as
swiftly as the evening shadows. I am withering
away like grass. But you, O LORD,
will sit on your throne forever. Your fame
will endure to every generation.

PSALM 102:1–7, 11–12

You are close to the brokenhearted,
you rescue those whose spirits are crushed.

PSALM 34:18*

You keep track of all my sorrows.
You have collected all my tears in your bottle.
You have recorded each one in your book.

PSALM 56:8

Let your unfailing love surround me, LORD,
for my hope is in you alone.

PSALM 33:22*

When You're Tempted

O LORD, listen to my cry; give me the discerning mind you promised. Listen to my prayer; rescue me as you promised. Let praise flow from my lips, for you have taught me your decrees. Let my tongue sing about your word, for all your commands are right. Give me a helping hand, for I have chosen to follow your commandments. O LORD, I have longed for your rescue, and your instructions are my delight. Let me live so I can praise you, and may your regulations help me. I have wandered away like a lost sheep; come and find me, for I have not forgotten your commands.

PSALM 119:169–176

Teach me your ways, O LORD, that I may live
according to your truth! Grant me purity of
heart, so that I may honor you. With all my
heart I will praise you, O Lord my God.
I will give glory to your name forever,
for your love for me is very great. You have
rescued me from the depths of death.

PSALM 86:11–13

Teach me how to live, O LORD. Lead me along
the right path, for my enemies are waiting
for me. Yet I am confident I will see the LORD's
goodness while I am here in the land of the living.

PSALM 27:11, 13

When You Need to Watch What You Say

O Lord, I am calling to you. Please hurry!
Listen when I cry to you for help! Accept my
prayer as incense offered to you, and my
upraised hands as an evening offering.
Take control of what I say, O Lord, and guard
my lips. Don't let me drift toward evil or take
part in acts of wickedness. Don't let me share
in the delicacies of those who do wrong.
Let the godly strike me! It will be a kindness!
If they correct me, it is soothing medicine.
Don't let me refuse it.

PSALM 141:1–5

How can I know all the sins lurking in my
heart? Cleanse me from these hidden faults.
Keep your servant from deliberate sins!
Don't let them control me. Then I will be free
of guilt and innocent of great sin. May the
words of my mouth and the meditation of
my heart be pleasing to you, O LORD, my rock
and my redeemer.

PSALM 19:12–14

I am determined not to sin in what I say.

PSALM 17:3

When I discovered your words,
I devoured them. They are my joy and
my heart's delight, for I bear your name,
O LORD God of Heaven's Armies.

JEREMIAH 15:16

When You're Wrestling with Pride and Envy

I almost lost my footing. My feet were slipping, and I was almost gone. For I envied the proud when I saw them prosper despite their wickedness. They seem to live such painless lives; their bodies are so healthy and strong. They don't have troubles like other people; they're not plagued with problems like everyone else. They wear pride like a jeweled necklace and clothe themselves with cruelty. These fat cats have everything their hearts could ever wish for! They scoff and speak only evil; in their pride they seek to crush others. They boast against the very heavens, and their words strut throughout the earth. Then I realized that my heart was bitter, and I was all torn up inside. I was so foolish and ignorant—I must have seemed like a senseless animal to you.

PSALM 73:2-9, 21-22

To the faithful you show yourself faithful;
to those with integrity you show integrity.
To the pure you show yourself pure, but to the
crooked you show yourself shrewd. You rescue
the humble, but you humiliate the proud.

PSALM 18:25–27

O God, you take no pleasure in wickedness;
you cannot tolerate the sins of the wicked.
Therefore, the proud may not stand
in your presence.

PSALM 5:4–5

Though the LORD is great, he cares for the
humble, but he keeps his distance from the
proud. The LORD will work out his plans
for my life—for your faithful love, O LORD,
endures forever. Don't abandon me,
for you made me.

PSALM 138:6, 8

When You're Struggling with Sexual Temptation

I will sing of your love and justice, LORD.
I will praise you with songs. I will be careful
to live a blameless life—when will you come
to help me? I will lead a life of integrity in
my own home. I will refuse to look at anything
vile and vulgar. I hate all who deal crookedly;
I will have nothing to do with them.
I will reject perverse ideas and stay away from
every evil. I will not tolerate people who
slander their neighbors. I will not endure
conceit and pride. I will search for faithful
people to be my companions.

PSALM 101:1–6

How can a young person stay pure?
By obeying your word. I have tried hard
to find you—don't let me wander from your
commands. I have hidden your word in
my heart, that I might not sin against you.
I will study your commandments and reflect
on your ways. I will delight in your decrees
and not forget your word.

PSALM 119:9–11, 15–16

Create in me a clean heart, O God.
Renew a loyal spirit within me. Do not banish
me from your presence, and don't take your
Holy Spirit from me. Restore to me the joy of
your salvation, and make me willing to obey you.

PSALM 51:10–12

When You Need to Be Reminded of God's Strength

Powerful is your arm! Strong is your hand!
Your right hand is lifted high in glorious
strength. Righteousness and justice are the
foundation of your throne. Unfailing love
and truth walk before you as attendants.
Happy are those who hear the joyful call to
worship, for they will walk in the light of your
presence, LORD. They rejoice all day long in
your wonderful reputation. They exult in your
righteousness. You are their glorious strength.
It pleases you to make us strong.

PSALM 89:13–17

LORD, you are my strength and fortress,
my refuge in the day of trouble!

JEREMIAH 16:19

Your right hand, O LORD, is glorious in power.
Your right hand, O LORD, smashes the enemy.
In the greatness of your majesty, you overthrow
those who rise against you. You unleash your
blazing fury; it consumes them like straw.

EXODUS 15:6–7

You have taught children and infants to
tell of your strength, silencing your enemies
and all who oppose you.

PSALM 8:2

When You Need Encouragement to Trust God

A single day in your courts is better than a
thousand anywhere else! I would rather be
a gatekeeper in the house of my God than live
the good life in the homes of the wicked.
For the LORD God is our sun and our shield.
You give us grace and glory. The LORD will
withhold no good thing from those who
do what is right. O LORD of Heaven's Armies,
what joy for those who trust in you.

PSALM 84:10–12*

O Lord, you alone are my hope. I've trusted you, O Lord, from childhood. Yes, you have been with me from birth; from my mother's womb you have cared for me. No wonder I am always praising you!

PSALM 71:5–6

I pray that God, the source of hope, will fill me completely with joy and peace because I trust in him. Then I will overflow with confident hope through the power of the Holy Spirit.

ROMANS 15:13*

I trust in your unfailing love.

PSALM 13:5

When You Need to Know That God Is with You

I can never escape from your Spirit!
I can never get away from your presence!
If I go up to heaven, you are there; if I go
down to the grave, you are there. If I ride the
wings of the morning, if I dwell by the farthest
oceans, even there your hand will guide me,
and your strength will support me. I could ask
the darkness to hide me and the light around
me to become night—but even in darkness
I cannot hide from you. To you the night
shines as bright as day. Darkness and
light are the same to you.

PSALM 139:7–12

How will anyone know that you look favorably
on me—on me and on your people—
if you don't go with us? For your presence
among us sets your people and me apart from
all other people on the earth.

EXODUS 33:16

You are the God who sees me.

GENESIS 16:13

LORD, be merciful to me, for I have waited
for you. Be my strong arm each day and
my salvation in times of trouble.

ISAIAH 33:2*

When You're Trying to Do What Is Right

O LORD, you are righteous, and your
regulations are fair. Your laws are perfect and
completely trustworthy. Your promises have
been thoroughly tested; that is why I love
them so much. Your justice is eternal,
and your instructions are perfectly true.
As pressure and stress bear down on me,
I find joy in your commands. Your laws
are always right; help me to understand
them so I may live.

PSALM 119:137–138, 140, 142–144

May the Lord my God show me
his approval and make my efforts successful.
Yes, make my efforts successful!

PSALM 90:17*

Your laws are my treasure; they are my heart's delight. I am determined to keep your decrees to the very end.

PSALM 119:111–112

To the faithful you show yourself faithful; to those with integrity you show integrity. To the pure you show yourself pure, but to the crooked you show yourself shrewd.

2 SAMUEL 22:26–27

May integrity and honesty protect me, for I put my hope in you.

PSALM 25:21

O LORD, God of Israel, there is no God like you in all of heaven above or on the earth below. You keep your covenant and show unfailing love to all who walk before you in wholehearted devotion.

1 KINGS 8:23

When the Wicked Seem to Win

Look at these wicked people— enjoying a life
of ease while their riches multiply. Did I keep
my heart pure for nothing? Did I keep myself
innocent for no reason? I get nothing but
trouble all day long; every morning brings me
pain. If I had really spoken this way to others,
I would have been a traitor to your people.
So I tried to understand why the wicked
prosper. But what a difficult task it is! Then I
went into your sanctuary, O God, and I finally
understood the destiny of the wicked.
Truly, you put them on a slippery path and
send them sliding over the cliff to destruction.
In an instant they are destroyed, completely
swept away by terrors. When you arise,
O Lord, you will laugh at their silly ideas as
a person laughs at dreams in the morning.

PSALM 73:12–20

LORD, you always give me justice when I bring
a case before you. So let me bring you this
complaint: Why are the wicked so prosperous?
Why are evil people so happy? You have
planted them, and they have taken root and
prospered. Your name is on their lips, but you
are far from their hearts.

JEREMIAH 12:1–2

Why do the wicked get away with despising
God? They think, "God will never call us to
account." But you see the trouble and grief
they cause. You take note of it and punish
them. The helpless put their trust in you.
You defend the orphans.

PSALM 10:13–14

Arise, O LORD! Do not let mere mortals
defy you! Judge the nations! Make them
tremble in fear, O LORD. Let the nations
know they are merely human.

PSALM 9:19–20

When You're Exhausted

Oh, that I had wings like a dove; then I would fly away and rest! I would fly far away to the quiet of the wilderness. O God, listen to my cry! Hear my prayer! From the ends of the earth, I cry to you for help when my heart is overwhelmed. Lead me to the towering rock of safety, for you are my safe refuge, a fortress where my enemies cannot reach me. Let me live forever in your sanctuary, safe beneath the shelter of your wings!

PSALM 55:6–7; 61:1–4

I cry out to the LORD; I plead for the
LORD's mercy. I pour out my complaints before
you and tell you all my troubles. When I am
overwhelmed, you alone know the way
I should turn.

PSALM 142:1–3*

Hold me up, and I shall be safe.

PSALM 119:117 NKJV

O my Strength, I will watch for you,
for you, O God, are my fortress.

PSALM 59:9 ESV

When You're Growing Older

And now, in my old age, don't set me aside.
Don't abandon me when my strength is failing.
O God, don't stay away. My God, please hurry
to help me. But I will keep on hoping for
your help; I will praise you more and more.
I will tell everyone about your righteousness.
All day long I will proclaim your saving power,
though I am not skilled with words. I will
praise your mighty deeds, O Sovereign LORD.
I will tell everyone that you alone are just.
Let me proclaim your power to this
new generation, your mighty miracles
to all who come after me.

PSALM 71:9, 12, 14–16, 18

Remember, O Lord, your compassion
and unfailing love, which you have shown
from long ages past. Do not remember the
rebellious sins of my youth. Remember me in
the light of your unfailing love, for you
are merciful, O Lord.

PSALM 25:6-7

Give me gladness in proportion to my former
misery! Replace the evil years with good.
Let me, your servant, see you work again;
let my children see your glory.

PSALM 90:15-16*

Lord, through all the generations you
have been our home! Before the mountains
were born, before you gave birth to the
earth and the world, from beginning to end,
you are God.

PSALM 90:1-2

When You Need to Remember God in a Challenging Time

You don't let me sleep. I am too distressed
even to pray! I think of the good old days,
long since ended, when my nights were filled
with joyful songs. I search my soul and ponder
the difference now. Has the Lord rejected me
forever? Will you never again be kind to me?
Is your unfailing love gone forever?
Have your promises permanently failed?
Has God forgotten to be gracious? Have you
slammed the door on your compassion?
But then I recall all you have done, O LORD;
I remember your wonderful deeds of long ago.
They are constantly in my thoughts. I cannot
stop thinking about your mighty works.
O God, your ways are holy. Is there any god
as mighty as you?

PSALM 77:4–9, 11–13*

Your name, O LORD, endures forever; your
fame, O LORD, is known to every generation.
For the LORD will give justice to his people
and have compassion on his servants.

PSALM 135:13–14

Once again you will have compassion on us.
You will trample our sins under your feet and
throw them into the depths of the ocean!
You will show us your faithfulness and
unfailing love as you promised to our
ancestors Abraham and Jacob long ago.

MICAH 7:19–20

You have the words that give eternal life.
I believe, and I know you are the
Holy One of God.

JOHN 6:68–69*

When You Need to Be Reminded That God Will Watch over You

O Lord, you have examined my heart and know everything about me. You know when I sit down or stand up. You know my thoughts even when I'm far away. You see me when I travel and when I rest at home. You know everything I do. You know what I am going to say even before I say it, Lord. You go before me and follow me. You place your hand of blessing on my head. Such knowledge is too wonderful for me, too great for me to understand!

PSALM 139:1–6

There is no one like the God of Israel.
You ride across the heavens to help me, across
the skies in majestic splendor. The eternal God
is my refuge, and your everlasting arms
are under me.

DEUTERONOMY 33:26–27*

But as for me, LORD, you know my heart.
You see me and test my thoughts.

JEREMIAH 12:3

I thank you, O God! I give thanks
because you are near. People everywhere
tell of your wonderful deeds.

PSALM 75:1*

Prayers
for Help

When You're Afraid

My enemies will retreat when I call to you for
help. This I know: God is on my side!
I praise you for what you have promised;
yes, I praise the LORD for what he has
promised. I trust in God, so why should I be
afraid? What can mere mortals do to me? For
you have rescued me from death; you have
kept my feet from slipping. So now I can walk
in your presence, O God, in your life-giving
light.

PSALM 56:9–11, 13*

Listen to my prayer, O God. Do not ignore
my cry for help! Please listen and answer me,
for I am overwhelmed by my troubles.
My heart pounds in my chest. The terror
of death assaults me. Fear and trembling
overwhelm me, and I can't stop shaking.

PSALM 55:1–2, 4–5

Keep me safe, my God, for in you I take refuge.

PSALM 16:1 NIV

When I am afraid, I put my trust in you.
In God, whose word I praise, in God I trust;
I shall not be afraid.

PSALM 56:3–4 ESV

When You're in Trouble

O LORD, I have come to you for protection;
don't let me be disgraced. Save me, for you do
what is right. Turn your ear to listen to me;
rescue me quickly. Be my rock of protection,
a fortress where I will be safe. You are my
rock and my fortress. For the honor of your
name, lead me out of this danger. Pull me
from the trap my enemies set for me, for I find
protection in you alone. I entrust my spirit
into your hand. Rescue me, LORD, for you
are a faithful God.

PSALM 31:1–5

Rescue me from the mud; don't let me sink any deeper! Save me from those who hate me, and pull me from these deep waters. Don't let the floods overwhelm me, or the deep waters swallow me, or the pit of death devour me.

PSALM 69:14–15

Don't hide from your servant; answer me quickly, for I am in deep trouble!

PSALM 69:17

Please, God, rescue me! Come quickly, LORD, and help me. May all who search for you be filled with joy and gladness in you. May those who love your salvation repeatedly shout, "God is great!" But as for me, I am poor and needy; please hurry to my aid, O God.
You are my helper and my savior;
O LORD, do not delay.

PSALM 70:1, 4–5

When You Need Direction

O LORD, I give my life to you. No one who
trusts in you will ever be disgraced,
but disgrace comes to those who try to deceive
others. Show me the right path, O LORD;
point out the road for me to follow.
Lead me by your truth and teach me,
for you are the God who saves me.
All day long I put my hope in you.

PSALM 25:1, 3–5

Send out your light and your truth;
let them guide me. Your word is a lamp to
guide my feet and a light for my path.

PSALM 43:3; 119:105

Lead me in the right path, O LORD.
Make your way plain for me to follow.

PSALM 5:8

Please, LORD, please save me.
Please, LORD, please give me success.

PSALM 118:25*

We do not know what to do,
but our eyes are on you.

2 CHRONICLES 20:12 ESV

What should I do, Lord?

ACTS 22:10

When You're Desperate for an Answer

I pray with all my heart; answer me, LORD!
I will obey your decrees. I cry out to you;
    rescue me, that I may obey your laws.
I rise early, before the sun is up; I cry out for
help and put my hope in your words. I stay
awake through the night, thinking about your
promise. In your faithful love, O LORD, hear
    my cry. I pray to you, O LORD, my rock.
Do not turn a deaf ear to me. Listen to my
prayer for mercy as I cry out to you for help,
as I lift my hands toward your holy sanctuary.

PSALM 119:145-149; 28:1-2

O LORD, how long will you forget me? Forever?
How long will you look the other way?
How long must I struggle with anguish in my
soul, with sorrow in my heart every day?
Turn and answer me, O LORD my God!

PSALM 13:1–3

Hear me as I pray, O LORD. Be merciful and
answer me! Do not turn your back on me.
Do not reject your servant in anger. You have
always been my helper. Don't leave me now;
don't abandon me, O God of my salvation!
Even if my father and mother abandon me,
the LORD will hold me close.

PSALM 27:7, 9–10

When You Need Wisdom to Follow the Lord

Your laws are wonderful. No wonder I obey
them! The teaching of your word gives light,
so even the simple can understand.
I pant with expectation, longing for your
commands. Come and show me your mercy,
as you do for all who love your name.
Guide my steps by your word, so I will not be
overcome by evil. Look upon me with love;
teach me your decrees.

PSALM 119:129–133, 135

Give me understanding and I will obey your
instructions; I will put them into practice with
all my heart. Make me walk along the path of
your commands, for that is where
my happiness is found.

PSALM 119:34–35

Teach me to do your will, for you are my God.
May your gracious Spirit lead me forward
on a firm footing.

PSALM 143:10

I will follow you wherever you go.

LUKE 9:57

When You Need to Be Protected from Harm

O LORD, I have come to you for protection;
don't let me be disgraced. Save me and
rescue me, for you do what is right. Turn your
ear to listen to me, and set me free.
Be my rock of safety where I can always hide.
Give the order to save me, for you are my rock
and my fortress. My God, rescue me from the
power of the wicked, from the clutches of cruel
oppressors. O LORD, rescue me from
evil people. Protect me from those who are
violent, those who plot evil in their hearts and
stir up trouble all day long. Their tongues
sting like a snake; the venom of a viper
drips from their lips.

PSALM 71:1–4; 140:1–3

I come to you for protection, O LORD my God.
Save me from my persecutors—rescue me!

PSALM 7:1

But you, LORD, are a shield around me,
my glory, the One who lifts my head high.
I call out to the LORD, and he answers me from
his holy mountain. I lie down and sleep;
I wake again, because the LORD sustains me.
I will not fear though tens of thousands
assail me on every side.

PSALM 3:3–6 NIV

When You Want to Ask God to Heal You

Have compassion on me, LORD, for I am weak.
Heal me, LORD, for my bones are in agony.
I am sick at heart. How long, O LORD, until
you restore me? Return, O LORD, and rescue
me. Save me because of your unfailing love.

PSALM 6:2–4

Jesus, Son of David, have mercy on me!

MARK 10:47

I am suffering and in pain.
Rescue me, O God, by your saving power.

PSALM 69:29

O LORD, if you heal me,
I will be truly healed; if you save me,
I will be truly saved.
My praises are for you alone!

JEREMIAH 17:14

If you are willing, you can heal me.

MARK 1:40

When You've Been Mistreated

I look for someone to come and help me,
but no one gives me a passing thought!
No one will help me; no one cares a bit what
happens to me. Then I pray to you, O Lord.
I say, "You are my place of refuge. You are all I
really want in life. Hear my cry, for I am very
low. Rescue me from my persecutors,
for they are too strong for me."

PSALM 142:4–6

How long, O Lord, will you look on and do
nothing? Rescue me from their fierce attacks.
Protect my life from these lions!

PSALM 35:17

Have mercy on me, LORD, have mercy,
for I have had my fill of contempt. I have had
more than my fill of the scoffing of the proud
and the contempt of the arrogant.

PSALM 123:3-4*

Rescue me, O LORD, from liars and
from all deceitful people.

PSALM 120:2

LORD, who can compare with you?
Who else rescues the helpless from the strong?
Who else protects the helpless and poor from
those who rob them?

PSALM 35:10

When You Need to Be Delivered from Your Enemies

Declare me innocent, O God! Defend me against these ungodly people. Rescue me from these unjust liars. For you are God, my only safe haven. Why have you tossed me aside? Why must I wander around in grief, oppressed by my enemies?

PSALM 43:1–2

Don't leave me to the mercy of my enemies, for I have done what is just and right. Please guarantee a blessing for me. Don't let the arrogant oppress me!

PSALM 119:121–122

Come and redeem me; free me from my
enemies. You know of my shame, scorn,
and disgrace. You see all that my enemies
are doing. Their insults have broken my heart,
and I am in despair.

PSALM 69:18–20

Rescue me from my enemies, LORD;
I run to you to hide me.

PSALM 143:9

Let your favor shine on your servant.
In your unfailing love, rescue me.

PSALM 31:16

When You Are in Distress

Save me, O God, for the floodwaters are up
to my neck. Deeper and deeper I sink into
the mire; I can't find a foothold. I am in deep
water, and the floods overwhelm me.
I am exhausted from crying for help;
my throat is parched. My eyes are swollen
with weeping, waiting for my God to help me.

PSALM 69:1–3

For the glory of your name, O LORD,
preserve my life. Because of your faithfulness,
bring me out of this distress.

PSALM 143:11

Do not abandon me, O LORD. Do not stand at
a distance, my God. Come quickly to help me,
O Lord my savior.

PSALM 38:21–22

O my God, lean down and listen to me.
Open your eyes and see my despair. I make this
plea, not because I deserve help, but because of
your mercy. O Lord, hear. O Lord, forgive.
O Lord, listen and act!

DANIEL 9:18–19*

When You Feel as if God Isn't Listening

O LORD, hear me as I pray; pay attention to
my groaning. Listen to my cry for help,
my King and my God, for I pray to no one but
you. Listen to my voice in the morning, LORD.
Each morning I bring my requests to you and
wait expectantly. I keep praying to you, LORD,
hoping this time you will show me favor.
In your unfailing love, O God, answer my
prayer with your sure salvation.

PSALM 5:1–3; 69:13

You, O Lord, are a God of compassion and
mercy, slow to get angry and filled with
unfailing love and faithfulness. Look down and
have mercy on me. Give your strength to your
servant; save me, the son of your servant.
Send me a sign of your favor.

PSALM 86:15–17

O LORD, God of Israel, you are enthroned
between the mighty cherubim! You alone are
God of all the kingdoms of the earth.
You alone created the heavens and the earth.
Bend down, O LORD, and listen! Open your eyes,
O LORD, and see!

2 KINGS 19:15–16

Hear me, LORD, and have mercy on me.
Help me, O LORD.

PSALM 30:10

When God Seems Far Away

My God, my God, why have you abandoned
me? Why are you so far away when I groan for
help? Every day I call to you, my God, but you
do not answer. Every night I lift my voice,
but I find no relief. Do not stay so far from
me, for trouble is near, and no one else can
help me. O LORD, do not stay far away!
You are my strength; come quickly to my aid!

PSALM 22:1–2, 11, 19

Remember your promise to me;
it is my only hope. Your promise revives me;
it comforts me in all my troubles.

PSALM 119:49–50

You have covered yourself with a cloud
so that no prayer can get through.

LAMENTATIONS 3:44 NIV

O LORD, why do you stand so far away?
Why do you hide when I am in trouble?

PSALM 10:1

Wake up, O Lord! Why do you sleep?
Get up! Do not reject me forever. Why do you
look the other way? Why do you ignore my
suffering and oppression? I collapse in the dust,
lying face down in the dirt. Rise up! Help me!
Ransom me because of your unfailing love.

PSALM 44:23–26*

When You've Been Falsely Accused

O God, whom I praise, don't stand silent and
aloof while the wicked slander me and tell lies
about me. They surround me with hateful
words and fight against me for no reason.
I love them, but they try to destroy me with
accusations even as I am praying for them!
They repay evil for good, and hatred for my
love. But deal well with me, O Sovereign LORD,
for the sake of your own reputation!
Rescue me because you are so faithful and good.
Help me, O LORD my God! Save me because
of your unfailing love. Let them see that this
is your doing, that you yourself have done it,
LORD. Then let them curse me if they like,
but you will bless me! When they attack me,
they will be disgraced! But I, your servant,
will go right on rejoicing!

PSALM 109:1–5, 21, 26–28

Malicious witnesses testify against me.
They accuse me of crimes I know nothing
about. They shout, "Aha! Aha! With our own
eyes we saw him do it!" O LORD, you know
all about this. Do not stay silent.
Do not abandon me now, O Lord.

PSALM 35:11, 21–22

Declare me innocent, O LORD, for I have
acted with integrity; I have trusted in the LORD
without wavering. Put me on trial, LORD, and
cross-examine me. Test my motives and my
heart. For I am always aware of your unfailing
love, and I have lived according to your truth.

PSALM 26:1–3

You hide me in the shelter of your presence,
safe from those who conspire against me.
You shelter me in your presence,
far from accusing tongues.

PSALM 31:20*

When You Need God to Fight for You

O LORD, oppose those who oppose me.
Fight those who fight against me. Put on your
armor, and take up your shield. Prepare for
battle, and come to my aid. Lift up your spear
and javelin against those who pursue me.
Let me hear you say, "I will give you victory!"
Rise up, O God, and scatter your enemies.
Let those who hate God run for their lives.
But let the godly rejoice. Let them be glad in
God's presence. Let them be filled with joy.

PSALM 35:1–3; 68:1,3

O LORD, the God of vengeance, O God of
vengeance, let your glorious justice shine forth!

PSALM 94:1

Come with great power, O God, and rescue
me! Defend me with your might. Listen to my
prayer, O God. Pay attention to my plea.

PSALM 54:1–2

Summon your might, O God. Display your
power, O God, as you have in the past.

PSALM 68:28

Have mercy on me, O God, have mercy!
I look to you for protection. I will hide
beneath the shadow of your wings until
the danger passes by.

PSALM 57:1

Though I am surrounded by troubles, you will
protect me from the anger of my enemies.

PSALM 138:7

When You've Been Oppressed

Hear my prayer, O LORD; listen to my plea!
Answer me because you are faithful and
righteous. Don't put your servant on trial,
for no one is innocent before you. My enemy
has chased me. He has knocked me to the
ground and forces me to live in darkness like
those in the grave. I am losing all hope;
I am paralyzed with fear. I remember the days
of old. I ponder all your great works and think
about what you have done. I lift my hands
to you in prayer. I thirst for you as parched
land thirsts for rain.

PSALM 143:1–6

You are a shelter for the oppressed,
a refuge in times of trouble.

PSALM 9:9*

Pour out your unfailing love on those who
love you; give justice to those with honest hearts.
Don't let the proud trample me or the wicked
push me around.

PSALM 36:10–11

Remember your covenant promises,
for the land is full of darkness and violence!
Don't let the downtrodden be humiliated
again. Instead, let the poor and needy
praise your name. Arise, O God,
and defend your cause.

PSALM 74:20–22

LORD, you know the hopes of the helpless.
Surely you will hear their cries and comfort
them. You will bring justice to the orphans
and the oppressed, so mere people can
no longer terrify them.

PSALM 10:17–18

When You Need God to Intervene

Oh, that you would burst from the heavens and come down! How the mountains would quake in your presence! As fire causes wood to burn and water to boil, your coming would make the nations tremble. Then your enemies would learn the reason for your fame! When you came down long ago, you did awesome deeds beyond our highest expectations. And oh, how the mountains quaked! For since the world began, no ear has heard and no eye has seen a God like you, who works for those who wait for him!

ISAIAH 64:1–4

Have mercy on me, O Lord, Son of David!
Lord, help me!

MATTHEW 15:22, 25

I am worn out waiting for your rescue,
but I have put my hope in your word.
My eyes are straining to see your promises come
true. When will you comfort me?

PSALM 119:81–82

Remember me, LORD, when you show favor
to your people; come near and rescue me.
Let me share in the prosperity of your chosen
ones. Let me rejoice in the joy of your people;
let me praise you with those who are your heritage.

PSALM 106:4–5

Open the heavens, LORD, and come down.

PSALM 144:5

When You Need Justice

O LORD, hear my plea for justice. Listen to my
cry for help. Pay attention to my prayer, for it
comes from honest lips. Declare me innocent,
for you see those who do right. You have tested
my thoughts and examined my heart in the
night. I have followed your commands, which
keep me from following cruel and evil people.
My steps have stayed on your path; I have not
wavered from following you. I am praying to
you because I know you will answer, O God.
Bend down and listen as I pray. Show me your
unfailing love in wonderful ways. By your
mighty power you rescue those who seek refuge
from their enemies. Guard me as you would
guard your own eyes. Hide me in the
shadow of your wings.

PSALM 17:1–8

O Lord, you are my lawyer! Plead my case!
For you have redeemed my life. You have seen
the wrong they have done to me; be my Judge,
to prove me right. You have seen the plots my
foes have laid against me.

LAMENTATIONS 3:58–60 TLB

Declare me righteous, O Lord, for I am
innocent, O Most High! End the evil of those
who are wicked, and defend the righteous.
For you look deep within the mind and heart,
O righteous God.

PSALM 7:8–9

Wake up! Rise to my defense! Take up my case,
my God and my Lord. Declare me not guilty,
O Lord my God, for you give justice.

PSALM 35:23–24

When There Is
Violence in the Land

How long, O Lord, must I call for help?
But you do not listen! "Violence is
everywhere!" I cry, but you do not come to
save. Must I forever see these evil deeds?
Why must I watch all this misery? Wherever I
look, I see destruction and violence.
I am surrounded by people who love to
argue and fight. The law has become paralyzed,
and there is no justice in the courts.
The wicked far outnumber the righteous,
so that justice has become perverted.

HABAKKUK 1:2–4

O LORD God of Heaven's Armies,
how long will you be angry with our prayers?
You have fed us with sorrow and made us
drink tears by the bucketful.

PSALM 80:4–5

If the LORD is with us, why has all this
happened to us? And where are all the
miracles our ancestors told us about?

JUDGES 6:13

I have heard all about you, LORD. I am filled
with awe by your amazing works. In this time
of our deep need, help us again as you did
in years gone by. And in your anger,
remember your mercy.

HABAKKUK 3:2

When God's People Are Persecuted

O God, do not be silent! Do not be deaf.
Do not be quiet, O God. Don't you hear the
uproar of your enemies? Don't you see that
your arrogant enemies are rising up?
They devise crafty schemes against your people;
they conspire against your precious ones.
O my God, scatter them like tumbleweed,
like chaff before the wind! As a fire burns a
forest and as a flame sets mountains ablaze,
chase them with your fierce storm; terrify them
with your tempest. Utterly disgrace them
until they submit to your name, O LORD.
Then they will learn that you alone are called
the LORD, that you alone are the Most High,
supreme over all the earth.

PSALM 83:1–3, 13–16, 18

The LORD's promises are pure, like silver
refined in a furnace, purified seven times over.
Therefore, LORD, we know you will protect the
oppressed, preserving them forever from this
lying generation, even though the wicked strut
about, and evil is praised throughout the land.

PSALM 12:6–8

Yet for your sake we face death all day long;
we are considered as sheep to be slaughtered.

PSALM 44:22 NIV

O LORD, protect your people
with your shepherd's staff; lead your flock,
your special possession.

MICAH 7:14

Prayers for
Blessings

When You Want to Ask God for a Miracle

O Sovereign LORD! You made the heavens and earth by your strong hand and powerful arm. Nothing is too hard for you! You are the great and powerful God, the LORD of Heaven's Armies. You have all wisdom and do great and mighty miracles. You performed miraculous signs and wonders in the land of Egypt— things still remembered to this day! And you have continued to do great miracles in Israel and all around the world. You have made your name famous to this day.

JEREMIAH 32:17, 18–20

You are the God of great wonders!
You demonstrate your awesome power
among the nations.

PSALM 77:14

Who is like you among the gods, O LORD—
glorious in holiness, awesome in splendor,
performing great wonders?

EXODUS 15:11

Stretch out your hand with healing power;
may miraculous signs and wonders be done
through the name of your holy servant Jesus.

ACTS 4:30

When You Want to
Ask God to Bless You

LORD, you are mine! I promise to obey your
words! With all my heart I want your blessings.
Be merciful as you promised. I pondered the
direction of my life, and I turned to follow
your laws. I will hurry, without delay, to obey
your commands. Evil people try to drag me
into sin, but I am firmly anchored to your
instructions. I am a friend to anyone who fears
you—anyone who obeys your commandments.
O LORD, your unfailing love fills the earth;
teach me your decrees.

PSALM 119:57–61, 63–64

Oh, that you would bless me. Let your hand
be with me, and keep me from harm.

1 CHRONICLES 4:10 NIV

Restore our fortunes, LORD, as streams renew
the desert. Those who plant in tears will
harvest with shouts of joy. They weep as they
go to plant their seed, but they sing as they
return with the harvest.

PSALM 126:4–6

May God be gracious to us and bless us
and make his face to shine upon us.

PSALM 67:1 ESV

I will not let you go unless you bless me.

GENESIS 32:26

When You Want God to Bless Someone to Know His Love

I fall to my knees and pray to the Father, the Creator of everything in heaven and on earth. I pray that from his glorious, unlimited resources he will empower you with inner strength through his Spirit. Then Christ will make his home in your hearts as you trust in him. Your roots will grow down into God's love and keep you strong. And may you have the power to understand, as all God's people should, how wide, how long, how high, and how deep his love is. May you experience the love of Christ, though it is too great to understand fully. Then you will be made complete with all the fullness of life and power that comes from God.

EPHESIANS 3:14–19

May God give you more and more mercy,
peace, and love.

JUDE 1:2

May the Lord make your love for one another
and for all people grow and overflow,
just as our love for you overflows. May he,
as a result, make your hearts strong, blameless,
and holy as you stand before God our Father
when our Lord Jesus comes again with
all his holy people. Amen.

1 THESSALONIANS 3:12–13

Peace be with you, and may God the Father
and the Lord Jesus Christ give you love with
faithfulness. May God's grace be eternally
upon all who love our Lord Jesus Christ.

EPHESIANS 6:23–24

When You Want God to Bless Someone to Know His Joy and Peace

May you be filled with joy, always thanking the Father. He has enabled you to share in the inheritance that belongs to his people, who live in the light. For he has rescued us from the kingdom of darkness and transferred us into the Kingdom of his dear Son, who purchased our freedom and forgave our sins.

COLOSSIANS 1:11–14

May you always be filled with the fruit of your salvation—the righteous character produced in your life by Jesus Christ —for this will bring much glory and praise to God.

PHILIPPIANS 1:11

May the LORD bless you and protect you.
May the LORD smile on you and be gracious
to you. May the LORD show you his favor
and give you his peace.

NUMBERS 6:24-26

May God give you more and more grace
and peace as you grow in your knowledge
of God and Jesus our Lord.

2 PETER 1:2

May the grace of our Lord Jesus Christ
be with your spirit.

GALATIANS 6:18

Now may the Lord of peace himself give
you peace at all times in every way.

2 THESSALONIANS 3:16 ESV

When You Want God to Bless Someone to Stand Strong in Faith

Now may the God of peace—who brought up from the dead our Lord Jesus, the great Shepherd of the sheep, and ratified an eternal covenant with his blood— may he equip you with all you need for doing his will. May he produce in you, through the power of Jesus Christ, every good thing that is pleasing to him. All glory to him forever and ever! Amen.

HEBREWS 13:20–21

May the Lord lead your hearts into a full understanding and expression of the love of God and the patient endurance that comes from Christ.

2 THESSALONIANS 3:5

May God give you the power to accomplish all the good things your faith prompts you to do. Then the name of our Lord Jesus will be honored because of the way you live, and you will be honored along with him. This is all made possible because of the grace of our God and our Lord, Jesus Christ.

2 THESSALONIANS 1:11–12*

Now may our Lord Jesus Christ himself and God our Father, who loved us and by his grace gave us eternal comfort and a wonderful hope, comfort you and strengthen you in every good thing you do and say.

2 THESSALONIANS 2:16–17

When You Want God to Bless Someone with a Happy Home

How joyful are those who fear the LORD—
all who follow his ways! You will enjoy the
fruit of your labor. How joyful and prosperous
you will be! Your wife will be like a fruitful
grapevine, flourishing within your home.
Your children will be like vigorous young olive
trees as they sit around your table. That is the
LORD's blessing for those who fear him.

PSALM 128:1–4

May the LORD richly bless both you and
your children. May you be blessed by the LORD,
who made heaven and earth.

PSALM 115:14–15

O LORD, do good to those who are good,
whose hearts are in tune with you.

PSALM 125:4

May the God who gives endurance and
encouragement give you the same attitude of
mind toward each other that Christ Jesus had,
so that with one mind and voice you
may glorify the God and Father of our
Lord Jesus Christ.

ROMANS 15:5–6 NIV

And now may God,
who gives us his peace, be with you.

ROMANS 15:33

When You Want God to Bless Your Nation

May our sons flourish in their youth like
well-nurtured plants. May our daughters be
like graceful pillars, carved to beautify a palace.
May our barns be filled with crops of every
kind. May the flocks in our fields multiply
by the thousands, even tens of thousands,
and may our oxen be loaded down with
produce. May there be no enemy breaking
through our walls, no going into captivity,
no cries of alarm in our town squares.
Yes, joyful are those who live like this!
Joyful indeed are those whose God is the LORD.

PSALM 144:12–15

May your land be blessed by the LORD with
the precious gift of dew from the heavens and
water from beneath the earth; with the rich
fruit that grows in the sun, and the rich harvest
produced each month; with the finest crops
of the ancient mountains, and the abundance
from the everlasting hills; with the best gifts of
the earth and its bounty, and the favor of the
one who appeared in the burning bush.

DEUTERONOMY 33:13–16*

May God the Father and Christ Jesus our
Lord give you grace, mercy, and peace.

1 TIMOTHY 1:2

Blessed is the nation whose God is the LORD.

PSALM 33:12 ESV

Acknowledgments

As you're reading these acknowledgments, would you do me a favor? Instead of just saying thanks, I'd like to ask you to please join me in praying for God's best blessings for each one mentioned here (I'm praying as I write) . . .

For Cari, my bride. Day after day, you go the distance and then some. I couldn't write my way out of a box without your practical gifts. I love you.

For Geoff and Stef. Thanks for understanding your dad's calling to write. May these books encourage you in faith, hope, and love.

For Dave Branon. Your editor's eye for detail, irrepressible humor, and friendship along the way have made this a better book, and made the writing of it even more of a pleasure.

For Miranda Gardner. Your vision for this project, generous guidance, faithful encouragement, and prayers for this writer are all priceless gifts from God.

For the entire team at Discovery House and Our Daily Bread Ministries. Your exemplary work for the gospel of Jesus Christ is an inspiration beyond words.

For our Peace Church family. Because of God's faithfulness, your faithfulness in prayer is bearing fruit in vital, unexpected ways all over the world.

And for you, the reader. May our loving Lord draw you ever nearer as you draw near to Him in prayer.

Scripture Index

OLD TESTAMENT

NEW TESTAMENT

Enjoy this book? Help us get the word out!

Share a link to the book or
mention it on social media

Write a review on your blog, on a retailer site,
or on our website (dhp.org)

Pick up another copy to share with someone

Recommend this book for your
church, book club, or small group

Follow Discovery House on
social media and join the discussion

Contact us to share your thoughts:

 @discoveryhouse   @DiscoveryHouse

Discovery House
P.O. Box 3566
Grand Rapids, MI 49501 USA

Phone: 1-800-653-8333
Email: books@dhp.org
Web: dhp.org